a coloring bo

American

Front cover: John Philip
Sousa; back: Duke Ellington;
& here: Leonard Bernstein.

By Eric Tomb & Paul Rail;
Covers by Donna Neary,
drawings by Nancy Conkle.

Composers

MW01153617

William Billings
1746-1800

The first Puritan settlers in New England took music very seriously. While they rejected many traditional church ceremonies, their reverence for the word of the Bible led them to make the group singing of psalms and hymns a central part of their own services. The *Bay Psalm Book* of 1640, which was the first book printed in the colonies, provided metrical versions of the Old Testament psalms which could be used for congregational singing. During the next century the often isolated country churches developed some very idiosyncratic singing styles.

A reform movement began around 1720. The reformers wanted to eliminate not only the irregularities but also the suggestion of license which had crept into church music. Armed with some of the first songbooks to include musical notation, itinerant singing masters then began to conduct singing schools throughout New England. But, while their instruction brought some regularity into the music of church services, it also aroused an interest in music for its own sake. If the students of the singing schools wanted to embellish the basic melodies of the psalms and hymns, they now had a clearer idea of how to do it; if they wanted to compose their own songs, they could now use the examples of their English contemporaries.

William Billings was the first American composer to develop under these conditions—he was certainly the first American composer to publish a substantial number of his own works—and his example influenced later American musicians and composers for nearly a century. Only fourteen when his Boston shopkeeper father died, he was forced to apprentice himself to a tanner and spent much of his life in that and other menial trades. Music provided not only a means to temporarily improve his station in life, but also an outlet for strong emotional tensions.

In spite of his imperfect education, Billings felt confident enough about his musical development to publish the first collection of original American songs, *The New-England Psalm-Singer*, when he was only twenty-four. Eight years later he brought out *The Singing Master's Assistant*, a mixture of his old and new songs which quickly became the most popular and influential musical text of its time. Most of the songs had geographical names ("Africa," "Brookfield," "Chester" and the like), which had little to do with their religious or patriotic lyrics and gave no hint of their fresh and forceful melodies.

Billings's success continued for several years after the end of the Revolution. In such collections as *The Suffolk Harmony*, *The Psalm-Singer's Amusement* and *The Continental Harmony*, he attempted larger and more complicated vocal effects than any American before him. At the same time he made several forays into humorous literature, satirizing both the musical and religious habits of his day. But the new American taste was turning toward simpler and less controversial styles. In the 1790s Billings had to make his meager living largely through non-musical work. His influence continued in the anthologies of pirated songs which later generations carried with them to the Western frontier.

William Billings

Francis Hopkinson
1737-1791

The generation that came of age in the years before the War of Independence may have been the most versatile group of men in American history. Though most of the leading revolutionaries were lawyers or merchants or gentleman farmers, many of them also shone as writers, scientists, architects, inventors, diplomats and political theorists. The signers of the Declaration of Independence included the famous polymaths Benjamin Franklin and Thomas Jefferson, the pioneering doctor Benjamin Rush and the lawyer-author-composer Francis Hopkinson.

To the new American nation Hopkinson figured most prominently as a jurist and a humorous writer; to a scattered band of intellectuals he appeared as a leader in the scientific, mathematical and technical development of the country; to his fellow Philadelphians he was one of the most important figures in the musical life of their city, though it was only late in his life that he openly declared himself as a composer.

The first student to enter the College of Philadelphia (later the University of Pennsylvania), which his lawyer father had helped found, Hopkinson displayed his wide ranging talents from the beginning of his career. Already an able harpsichordist and organist, he actively promoted several concerts for college and wider audiences and may have provided the music for some of the masques and oratorios which were performed while he was a student. As part of his musical studies, he recorded a number of his own songs in his notebook; years later he claimed that these had made him "the first native of the United States who has produced a Musical Composition," and indeed his "My days Have Been So Wondrous Free" is today considered the earliest known secular song written in America.

After graduating from the College in 1757, Hopkinson received a master's degree there in 1760, studied law, was admitted to the bar, moved to New Jersey and became active in local politics. An early supporter of the cause of independence, he was a member of the Continental Congress which approved the Declaration of Independence and helped supervise naval and financial matters during the war. As the nation began to take shape, he served as admiralty judge and then as federal district judge in Pennsylvania.

Through all this time, Hopkinson's artistic ventures kept pace with his religious and political interests. On the one hand he translated the Psalms from Dutch to English for church use and composed a tune for one of them. On the other hand he wrote sentimental and satirical poems, including the "Ballad of the Kegs," which mocked British conduct of the war and was "worth as much just then as the winning of a considerable battle."

After the war, Hopkinson continued to write poems and songs in between his judicial duties. In 1788 he published an elegant volume of *Seven Songs*, which he dedicated to George Washington and which included pieces dating back to 1759. Unlike the works of Billings and others, which were intended for church congregations and choral societies, these were to be performed individually to a keyboard accompaniment and represent the first "art songs" in American history.

Francis Hopkinson

Stephen Foster
1826-1864

By the middle of the nineteenth century music publishing in the United States was big business with fairly mechanical procedures. Publishers would rush into print the latest arias from the most popular European opera composers or endlessly recirculate the well-established hymns which church congregations always seemed to need. After 1830 or so they had a new source of material. Minstrel shows, in which whites in blackface imitated what they thought were the songs of African slaves, drew huge audiences in all the major cities. Sheet music of minstrel songs soon penetrated into even the smallest hamlets.

Growing up near Pittsburgh as it was developing from a small frontier town into a major industrial center, Stephen Foster experienced all the available kinds of music. The son of a leading merchant and politician, he was encouraged to appreciate art, music and literature—and discouraged from taking any of them too seriously. His marked talent for music, the ease with which he learned the guitar, banjo and other instruments and his strong affinity for minstrel songs all seemed like youthful enthusiasms which would soon take a backseat to his career in business.

Then he wrote "Oh! Susanna." It wasn't his first published song; it wasn't one he even gave much importance to. But it gained such huge success—becoming almost a folk song for the forty-niners on their way to the California gold fields—that it allowed Foster to leave his job bookkeeping for his brother's Cincinnati trading company and devote himself to songwriting. He signed contracts with several East Coast publishers, married, and began to turn out the most famous set of songs in American history.

But they didn't make him famous until years after his death. In the early 1850s, when he specialized in "Ethiopian" or dialect slave songs like "Old Folks at Home," "Massa's in de Cold, Cold Ground," "Camptown Races" and "Ring de Banjo," he sold the performance rights for many of them to the popular minstrel E. P. Christy and these first appeared under Christy's name. By the time he was well enough known that customers would buy an unfamiliar song because it bore his name, he had begun to run downhill.

Generous, emotional and impulsive, Foster had trouble dealing with financial matters; that made relations with his more conventional wife Jane difficult; that left him liable to drink too much. After 1855 the quality of his songs dropped drastically. He still composed minstrel-style slave songs (though no longer in dialect) and more generic "plantation" songs like the earlier "My Old Kentucky Home," but most of his energy went into largely uninspired sentimental ballads of early death and unrequited love.

In the decades before he died nearly destitute in New York City, Foster wrote only a few great songs (notably "Old Black Joe" and "Beautiful Dreamer"). Though he had by now lost most of the comic verve with which he had begun his career, his feel for simple, haunting melodies still occasionally ran at full strength.

Stephen Foster

Louis Moreau Gottschalk
1829-1869

American music has always been big-city music. Until the end of the nineteenth century, most of it derived from foreign, especially European, models, which entered the country through the great seaports of the eastern and Gulf coast states. From there it slowly seeped into the countryside, where generations of tinkering gradually gave it a distinctly American flavor. But the rural "folk music" that resulted only gained a following in the middle of the twentieth century; before that American audiences hankered for the kinds of music that urban theaters, concert-halls and publishers could provide.

Most of the East coast cities confined themselves to imitations of European fashions. But New Orleans, which still cherished memories of French and Spanish rule when Louis Moreau Gottschalk was born there, was also open to the African and Latin-American tradition which flourished along the Gulf coast and in the Caribbean. While aping European manners when on show, the *Orleanaises* could also relax into the southern styles when they wanted to unwind.

This unique mixture of cultural styles made New Orleans both more liberating and more confining than other American cities. Gottschalk, the son of an English father and a Creole mother, was the musical star of the city until he was thirteen. By then his prodigious piano playing had exhausted the local teaching resources and he moved on to Paris for advanced study. Unable as a foreigner to enter the famous *Conservatoire*, he trained with the best private teachers and began a spectacular career as a concert pianist while still in his teens.

He also began to compose. Vacationing in the French countryside between concert tours, Gottschalk started to fit the melodies he had heard from groups of African slaves back home into the contemporary piano style molded by Chopin and Liszt. At a time when ethnic or nationalistic music was still quite new (Chopin and Liszt were its chief exponents), pieces like "Bamboula" and "Le Bananier" created a sensation. They were, for most Europeans, the first hint that the mythical wilds of America could produce music worthy of their attention—and maybe even a bit in advance of their own.

After returning to the United States in 1853, Gottschalk continued to flourish both as a pianist and a composer. Some of the most successful pieces he wrote in this time were simply good examples of sentimental salon music. But his increasing love of Caribbean and Latin American music also led him to pattern some of his major orchestral works around the unusual rhythms and harmonies of the South.

While performing in California in 1865 Gottschalk became involved with a woman student; the affair was blown up into a scandal that forced him to flee the United States, never to return. He embarked on a concert tour of South America, organizing a series of "monster" concerts—sometimes involving hundreds of musicians and a dozen or more pianists—which spread his fame from city to city. He had just produced one of these in Rio de Janeiro, where he had made friends with the Emperor of Brazil, when he died suddenly of uncertain causes.

Louis Moreau Gottschalk

John Philip Sousa
1854-1932

Armies have always had bands of one sort or another. The blare of pipes and drums served to inspire soldiers marching into combat and to entertain them in the long dull periods between battles. But it was only with the rise of standing national armies during the seventeenth century that military bands took on an independent life of their own. By the middle of the nineteenth century, regimental bands performed at all kinds of public functions. In an era when the European nations fought very few wars, their military bands promoted patriotic sentiment and preserved a sense of potential national heroism. John Philip Sousa's United States Marine Band, probably the most famous and accomplished unit of its age, flourished at a time when American military forces had dwindled almost to nothingness.

Though it was the Marine Band that made Sousa famous, it was only a part of his wide-ranging musical life. The son of a Band trombonist, he was born in Washington, D.C. shortly before the Civil War, in time to experience the patriotic and musical fervor of the war years. As a child he studied the violin as well as the brasses, and was leading his own dance band when barely into his teens. At fourteen he joined the Marine Band himself, and three years later became its first trombonist. But he was shortly restless, and returned to civilian life.

Sousa now began to work in the theater, both as a violinist and conductor of musicals. When Jacques Offenbach, the French composer of light operas, visited Philadelphia to conduct at the Centennial Exposition there, Sousa joined his orchestra. Soon after he took on the position of conductor with a Gilbert and Sullivan company, and began to write his own comic opera. *Our Flirtation* was staged with a favorable reception in 1880, but the same year he was offered the conductorship of the United States Marine Band, and accepted.

When Sousa returned to the Marine Band, he found it in a sorry state. Within a few years he made it a highly disciplined, musically exciting organization, partly through his precise and energetic conducting, partly through the outstanding marches he wrote for it to perform. During the 1880s he composed "Semper Fidelis," "The Washington Post," "The Thunderer," and "High School Cadets." When he led the Band on a tour of Europe in 1890, the press began to call him "the March King."

In 1892 Sousa left the Marines to form his own military-style band, which performed over ten thousand concerts around the world in the next forty years. His enormous success not only made him a wealthy man, but also allowed him to expand into other areas, both musical (he wrote ten light operas—most notably *Desirée* in 1884 and *El Capitán* in 1896—plus many songs, waltzes and orchestral suites) and literary (two successful novels, an autobiography and numerous articles and sketches). The march nonetheless remained his greatest love and highest achievement. Of the over 130 marches he wrote during his life, some of the finest appeared after he left the Marine Band. He wrote "The Liberty Bell" in 1893, "King Cotton" in 1896 and "Hands Across the Sea" in 1899. He died of a heart attack shortly after conducting his most famous march, "The Stars and Stripes Forever," at the age of seventy-eight.

John Philip Sousa

Victor Herbert
1859-1924

In the summer of 1901 the New York magazine *Musical Courier* published a virulent attack on Victor Herbert, who was then conductor of the Pittsburgh Symphony Orchestra and a leading composer of light operas for the New York stage. The article claimed that Herbert's flair for popular music obliterated any talent he might have for interpreting the European symphonic classics, then undercut even his popular success by insisting that he had plagiarized almost all of his tunes.

When Herbert sued the editor of the *Musical Courier* for libel, his lawyers argued that his musical memory was so complete and so precise that he had a melody in his head for every possible situation and emotion; if some of them were similar to ones other composers had used in similar musical circumstances, it simply showed how well they fit their purpose. One witness claimed that his use of common themes served the same goal as beginning fairy tales with the phrase "Once upon a time..." Herbert won the case and went on to write his most popular works.

The suit drew attention to Herbert's unsurpassed strengths—and to his usually overlooked weaknesses. His musical range was so vast and so seemingly effortless— he was more or less the Leonard Bernstein of his time—that he found it easy to stretch himself too thin, often piecing together several stage or orchestral pieces at the same time and not always giving each piece the total attention it required. But even then his flair for melody and orchestration was so strong that he wrote more fine light operas than all his rivals put together and came closer than anyone else to writing a successful American grand opera.

Born in a prominent Dublin family (the famous Irish artist, writer and composer Samuel Lover was his mother's father), Herbert lost his father in early childhood. Mother and son resettled in Germany, where she remarried and he received a thorough education, turning to music after medicine proved too expensive. An accomplished cellist, he was rising rapidly as soloist, orchestral player and composer when the Metropolitan Opera Company called his wife, soprano Therese Foerster, to New York. After several years as cellist in the Metropolitan orchestra, he began to teach at the new National Conservatory of Music, where he was an active collaborator of Antonín Dvořák, while continuing to compose and conduct.

But Herbert found a faster road to fame and fortune—both of which delighted him—in light music. In 1893 he became conductor of the popular Gilmore's band, which toured widely, and later of the Victor Herbert Orchestra. At about the same time he began to write the first of his forty-some light operas. From 1895 to 1915 such shows of his as *Babes in Toyland*, *The Fortune Teller*, *Mlle Modiste* and *Naughty Marietta* almost completely dominated the American stage.

As public taste began to change in the 1910s, Herbert returned to more serious music, producing the briefly popular operas *Natoma* and *Madeleine*. But his greatest success came after his death, as radio and phonographs spread his songs into all parts of the country, making them classics of American popular music.

Victor Herbert

Edward MacDowell
1861-1908

By the end of the nineteenth century, American musicians had begun to win some respect from their European colleagues. When he went to Paris to study music in 1876, the fifteen-year-old Edward MacDowell easily gained admission to the *Conservatoire* which had earlier rejected Gottschalk. He went on to study in the conservatories of Stuttgart and Frankfurt in Germany and began to teach piano at the Darmstadt conservatory when he was only twenty. A protégé of the well-known composer Joachim Raff, he also received encouraging words from both Franz Liszt and Edvard Grieg.

Although MacDowell first drew notice as a pianist and continued to perform publicly for most of his life, he gradually came to regard himself primarily as a composer, working in the extravagant late-Romantic style which then dominated European music. Gifted with a vivid visual sense (he could easily have made a career as an artist), he was also strongly attracted to narrative poetry and northern European folklore. It was natural that his first mature works would be musical descriptions of physical scenes (usually landscapes) or tone poems which tried to convey the progress of a specific story. In these pieces he adapted the style of "program" or descriptive music which Liszt and Wagner had first made fashionable and which reached its culmination in the works of Richard Strauss and Debussy.

While he remained in Europe, MacDowell produced several impressive orchestral works. Besides the two Grieg-like piano concertos, he finished two tone poems, *Lancelot and Elaine*, based on Arthurian legend, and *Hamlet and Ophelia*, based on Shakespeare, and began to fashion Keats's poem *Lamia* into a third. They all received an enthusiastic reception both in Europe and America; when MacDowell returned home in 1888, he found that critics were already beginning to treat him as the most important American composer.

The praise continued for the rest of his life, but praise was never enough to pay his bills. After a few years teaching privately in Boston, MacDowell became the first professor of music at New York's Columbia University in 1896. Since his job involved not only teaching a number of classes, but also creating a new department from scratch, hiring and training other professors, he had little time left for writing his own music. But he made a practice of adding at least a few bars every day to his sketchbook, then reworking them during the summer at the farm he had bought in Peterborough, New Hampshire.

Yet in the twenty years which remained to him in America, MacDowell wrote only two large orchestral works; these were based on American scenes and stories rather than European models. As he readjusted to his native land, he found his personal voice in mostly small-scale piano pieces, choral works and songs. *Woodland Sketches*, *Sea Pieces* and *New England Idyls*, all written in the decade before he died of a brain lesion at forty-seven, hinted at what could have become a distinctly American style of classical music.

After his death, MacDowell's Peterborough farm became a retreat where promising American writers and artists can work in supportive seclusion.

Edward MacDowell

Scott Joplin
1868-1917

The blackface minstrel shows had always gained much of their appeal from the banjo music they featured. Though it was the only instrument invented in the young United States, the banjo was based on West African models and lent itself easily to the irregular, syncopated rhythms of African music.

In the difficult years after the Civil War, the ex-slaves and their children frequently found their chief solace in their own music. For the poorer groups, this would usually consist of songs with African-style melodies and harmonies, with perhaps a simple banjo or guitar accompaniment. The more prosperous and sophisticated blacks, who usually lived in the larger Southern towns, aspired to the European forms that still dominated American culture, going all out to master European marches and dances on pianos and wind instruments. But even there African rhythms cropped up and a strong note of mockery sometimes crept into their imitations: the strutting "cakewalks" which first became popular among Florida blacks in the 1870s seemed to ridicule the pompous stiffness of upper-class whites. This ambivalent mixture of European melodic forms and African rhythms soon produced the completely original styles of ragtime and jazz, as the more purely African singing gave rise to gospel music and the blues.

Scott Joplin spent the first half of his life sorting through all these musical forms, the second half crystallizing one of them better than anyone else. The son of a railroad laborer, he grew up in Texarkana, Texas, where musical opportunities were few. His was a musical family and he gained a basic mastery of the piano before leaving home at fourteen when his father insisted he follow a more reliable career. After making his way as pianist in disreputable establishments up and down the Mississippi, he settled west of St. Louis and published his first compositions.

A few sentimental songs, marches and waltzes followed before Joplin struck gold in 1898 with the "Maple Leaf Rag," a piano piece which made both him and ragtime famous. In it he formalized the music he had learned during his apprenticeship, in which banjo-style syncopation overlay the repetitive structure of European marches and dances to produce a melody both lively and contemplative. Pieces like "Elite Syncopations," "The Entertainer," "The Cascades" and "Gladiolus Rag" confirmed him as the most accomplished composer in an increasingly popular field.

By 1910 ragtime had become a national craze, and white composers like Irving Berlin scored huge hits with very loose versions of the original style. Joplin never took to these innovations. While he had long wanted to extend ragtime into opera, ballet and other "respectable" forms , he always insisted on sticking to the original rhythms and structure. His opera *Treemonisha*, which he wrote as his health was beginning to fail, never got beyond one rehearsal. In the years after his death, jazz replaced ragtime as the reigning musical fad. It was only in the late 1960s that large audiences rediscovered the limpid expressiveness of his music.

Maple Leaf Rag

COMPOSED BY

SCOTT JOPLIN.

PRICE 50¢

SEDALIA, Mo.

Charles Ives
1874-1954

Charles Ives always insisted that music should be an outgrowth of everyday life. "Every man," he once hopefully predicted, "while digging his potatoes, will breathe his own Epics, his own Symphonies." And he would do it in a vigorous American manner, celebrating independence and initiative while still remaining true to the spirit and tradition of the land and its people.

Many turn-of-the-century American composers would probably have echoed Ives's beliefs. But no one else could possibly have understood what he meant by independence or tradition. The way he transmuted the sounds and values of history into a music of the future was so tied into his personal experiences that it baffled all his contemporaries. It was only many decades later, after other composers had repeated his experiments, that his music began to make sense to the general public.

Most of Ives's music was an earnest attempt to recreate the sounds and feelings he had experienced in and around his childhood hometown of Danbury, Connecticut. The very idiosyncratic, experimental way he put his music together also stemmed from his childhood, from the example of the father he idolized. George Ives had been an army bandmaster during the Civil War and then returned to teach music and lead the local band. George taught his son the accepted rules of music, but also encouraged him to "stretch his ears" and experiment with new instruments, new tonal relationships and new ideas of what kinds of sounds constituted music. He would sometimes have him sing a song in one key while accompanying him in another.

A talented athlete as well as musician, Ives took his very physical, anti-dogmatic approach to music on to Yale, where he won the interest, if not the encouragement, of traditional teachers like Horatio Parker. But while he was determined to carry on his father's experiments, he refused to limit himself as his father had done by depending on his music for his living. His New York insurance agency, which he started with the odd mixture of pragmatism and idealism which marked all his activities, earned him a fortune and freed him to write the kind of music he pleased.

Until a heart attack greatly reduced his activity in 1918, Ives wrote a full array of symphonies, sonatas, concertos and chamber works in which he subjected the hymns, marches and popular songs of his boyhood to his unique musical vision. Working in almost total isolation, he composed pieces using several rhythms or keys at once or no key at all, combining many notes into dense clusters, arranging his notes in irregular patterns or just by chance. These were all techniques which later came to be associated with composers like Schönberg, Stravinsky, Milhaud, Cowell, Cage and others.

Ives's music remained almost unplayed—and when played almost always misunderstood—until the mid-1940s. Critical and public recognition came at last when he was in his seventies. In his last few years he found himself acclaimed the greatest and most original of American composers.

Charles Ives

The Second New England School

New England was the cradle of American music. Music historians sometimes refer to William Billings and the singing school masters who followed him as the First New England School. The most prominent American composers of a century later can be loosely grouped together as the Second New England School, or, as they are sometimes called, the Boston Classicists. That title indicates the center of their activity as well as their prevailing allegiance to Germanic musical models: the Viennese classicists, and, especially, Mendelssohn, Schumann and Brahms.

The founding father of this school was John Knowles Paine (1839-1806). Though his works are not widely heard today, he was a pivotal figure in American music, both as a composer and as an educator. Paine was born in Portland, Maine, the son of a bandleader and grandson of an organbuilder. He received the finest musical training locally available and was already an accomplished organist when, in 1858, he went to Germany for three years of study at the Berlin Hochschule. While abroad he met and played for Clara Schumann, the great concert pianist and widow of Robert Schumann. As an organist, he was also influenced by the great revival of interest in Bach then taking place.

Returning to America, Paine settled in Boston, where he played the organ, lectured, and began to compose. In 1862 he became the choir director and organist at Harvard's Appleton Chapel; he would be affiliated with the university for the rest of his life, writing over one hundred pieces for performance on the campus. In 1873, overcoming a decade of resistance from faculty traditionalists who considered music an unworthy academic discipline, he was appointed assistant professor of music, and full professor two years later. He proceeded to organize the first college department of music in America, and in the next three decades many future composers of distinction passed through his classes.

Our country's first professor of music was also the first American composer to work in the larger forms. His Mass in D of 1865 was acclaimed on both sides of the Atlantic. The oratorio *St. Peter* followed, and in 1875 Paine produced the first American symphony. Among his many other compositions *Overture to As You Like It* and incidental music to *Oedipus Tyrannus* of Sophocles stand out.

The most noteworthy of Paine's many pupils was Arthur Foote (1853-1937). A native of Salem, Massachusetts, he took piano lessons as a boy, but intended a career in law when he entered Harvard. He took Paine's courses though, and a summer of organ instruction after graduation determined him to pursue music. He returned to Harvard where he was awarded the first Master of Arts degree in music in the United States. He then set himself up as a private piano teacher in Boston, later teaching at the New England Conservatory, and served for over thirty years as organist at the First Unitarian Church. In 1881 Foote began to publish his compositions. He wrote many choral works and songs, but it is his orchestral works and chamber pieces that are remembered today. The latter, such as his two lyrical piano trios, have a strong Brahmsian flavor. Of the former, his Suite in E for strings has maintained a position in the standard repertoire. *A Night Piece*, his most popular work, was written for flute and string quartet, but orchestrated at the request of the

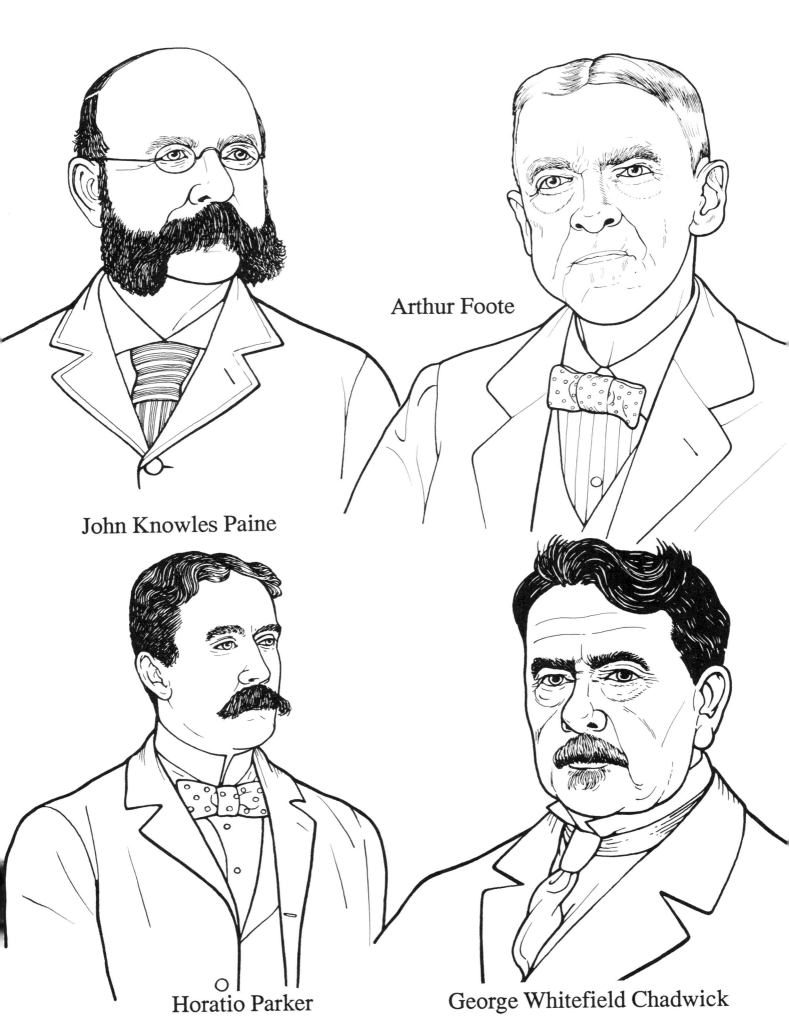

Arthur Foote

John Knowles Paine

Horatio Parker

George Whitefield Chadwick

conductor Pierre Monteux, who premiered the new version with the Boston Symphony in 1923. The same orchestra honored Foote with a special concert on the occasion of his eightieth birthday.

A year younger than Foote, George Whitefield Chadwick (1854-1931) did not go to Harvard. A high school dropout, this least patrician of the New England composers retained a lifelong pride in his birthplace of Lowell, Massachusetts, the unglamorous mill town famously disavowed by another native son, expatriate artist and dandy J. A. M. Whistler. Chadwick received his first music instruction from his older brother, and was playing church organ in his middle teens. Against the opposition of his father, a self-made businessman, he continued to study music, and in 1876 he secured a professorship at a Michigan college. In one year he saved enough to make the requisite pilgrimage to Germany, where while still a student he scored his first successes as a composer. Two string quartets were performed and well received, and an overture with a very American subject, *Rip Van Winkle*, won first prize in an annual concert at the Leipzig Conservatory. This triumph opened many doors for him upon his return home: as a composer, he was performed early and often, and as a teacher he was soon a major draw. In 1897 he became director of the New England Conservatory of Music; he modernized its curriculum, and, like Paine before him, was the mentor of a generation of composers.

Nearly every musical form is represented in Chadwick's considerable oeuvre. In keeping with the temper of the times, many of his works bore titles that alluded to classical mythology, and evoked nostalgia for a lost golden age. But at its best and most representative Chadwick's music has distinctly American elements. The scherzo of his Second Symphony incorporated a theme of African-American inspiration a decade before Dvořák did so in the symphony *From the New World*. And if his early, successful operetta *Tabasco* owed a debt to Gilbert and Sullivan, his most ambitious work was very much of its time and place. *The Padrone* is a grand opera set in the Italian immigrant community of Boston's North End. Chadwick was always interested in art and literature, and the libretto for *The Padrone* paralleled naturalistic developments in the novels of Theodore Dreiser and the paintings of the Ashcan School. Sadly, its gritty realism was too much for the Metropolitan Opera, and the rejection of Chadwick's magnum opus put a damper on the composition of opera in America for years to come.

When the young Chadwick opened a studio in Boston upon his return from Europe, one of his first students was a lad of seventeen named Horatio Parker. Parker (1863-1919), born in Auburndale, just west of Boston, had only become interested in music a few years before, but, with his mother as his first teacher, took to it with great zeal. In 1882 he went to Germany to finish his studies; back in the United States he settled for a time in New York. From 1892 to 1893 he taught counterpoint there at the National Conservatory, then under the direction of Antonín Dvořák. He composed his greatest work at this time for a conservatory competition. *Hora Novissima*, a cantata setting of a medieval Latin poem, made his reputation in America, and in England as well, where choral music was especially popular. Following a string of English commissions and festival performances, Parker was awarded a Doctor of Music from Cambridge University. In 1904 he became dean of Yale's music school, where he remained for the rest of his life, teaching among others

Amy Beach
1867-1944

Charles Ives and Roger Sessions. Meanwhile he directed a number of choral groups, and commuted to Boston and later New York to perform as church organist, still finding time to compose, concentrating as he always had on vocal music. In the decade before his premature death from pneumonia he wrote two operas, the first of which, *Mona*, set in ancient Roman Britain, was only the second by an American to be staged at the Metropolitan Opera.

Amy Beach (1867-1944), or Mrs. H. H. A. Beach, as she was known in her lifetime, was the first American woman to achieve international recognition as a composer. Born Amy Marcy Cheney in Henniker, New Hampshire, she showed musical talent quite early, composing for piano by the age of four. She studied with her mother, and then with private teachers in Boston, where her family had moved. She began performing at sixteen, and a year later made her début with the Boston Symphony Orchestra, playing Chopin's Concerto in F minor. But at eighteen she married a prominent Boston surgeon, and at his wish she cut short her concert career. Dr. Beach was a music lover, though, and encouraged Amy to compose. At first she wrote songs, then a cadenza for Beethoven's third Piano Concerto. She worked for three years on the Mass in E-flat, the first by an American women, and it was performed by the Boston Handel and Haydn Society. The following year she wrote on commission the *Festival Jubilate* for the dedication of the Woman's Building at the Colombian Exposition in Chicago. In 1896 Beach passed another milestone with her *Gaelic Symphony*, the first again by an American woman, and the first performed, by the Boston Symphony Orchestra. A large and technically assured work, it was a truly impressive accomplishment for a composer who had largely taught herself by analyzing scores. Beach continued to compose throughout her life, producing a major piano concerto, chamber music, and many songs, of which her settings of three poems by Robert Browning were especially popular. When her husband died in 1910, she went to Europe for four years, and resumed playing concerts.

By the time of Amy Beach's own death in 1944, the critical reputation of the New England composers had fallen on hard times. German influence on American culture, already in decline, went into eclipse with the advent of World War I. With the emergence of a vigorous nationalism in American music during the Depression years, they seemed increasingly irrelevant, and with the rise of serialism as a dominant musical force after World War II, they seemed to have been consigned to the dustbin of history. But the New England School has been reevaluated in recent years, with many pieces receiving their first recording. A new generation is coming to appreciate a body of work that, if conservative and backward-looking, displays consummate craftsmanship and a dedication to beauty.

The Growth of Jazz and Blues

At the start of the twentieth century European-American and African-American musical styles were blending in startling ways all over the country—mixing far more easily than the people they represented. Most of these conglomerations—the Florida cakewalk, the Mississippi Valley ragtime—created a quick sensation and then died away. The mix that occurred in New Orleans, a mix that had gotten a second, supercharged African element from the nearby Caribbean islands, travelled farther and longer. In a couple of decades it became jazz.

Exactly what that was was always hard to say, though anyone who heard the early jazz bands knew that they were playing something very different from the European-style dances and marches which were then the staple of popular music. Though the lower-class blacks who formed many of New Orleans's street bands had mastered the brass instruments and many of the pop tunes they would be expected to play at picnics or funerals, they gave their music a new kind of rhythm and a disconcerting harmony. The syncopated rhythm was close to the irregularity of ragtime, but with the added unpredictability that half a dozen separate instrumentalists almost guaranteed. The strange harmony came from the "blue notes," the flatted third and seventh notes of the octave—the result of trying to fit a five-note African scale into a seven-note European one.

The unusual scale the jazz bands used came directly from the blues songs, improvised lyrics strung on some standard twelve-bar melodies, which ex-slaves had begun to perform all over the South. From the blues singers the jazz players got the habit of improvising around a few set elements in their songs and also a totally new way of playing their instruments, distorting the normally clear tones of a trumpet or trombone to imitate the grunts and growls of a human voice. Well into the 1920s, it was simplest to say that jazz was instrumental blues.

The jazz style had already begun to spread by the start of World War I; when military authorities closed down the disreputable establishments of the Storyville section of New Orleans, where local musicians had found their work, they headed north and jazz soon established itself in St. Louis, Kansas City, Chicago, New York and Los Angeles. By this time what had begun as a fairly spontaneous folk art was beginning to take on a distinct, easily copied form which kept its broad outlines for the next twenty-five years. Composers like W. C. Handy ("St. Louis Blues," "Yellow Dog Blues" and many others) helped popularize the long, mournfully wailing tunes most people associate with the word "blues." Others like pianist Jelly Roll Morton ("Jelly Roll Blues," "King Porter Stomp," "Black Bottom Stomp") took the free-wheeling New Orleans-style band and molded it into a highly disciplined but still spontaneous group, in which each member got the chance for extended solos. By the mid-twenties soloists like trumpeter Louis Armstrong were becoming stars in their own right while bandleaders like Don Redman and Fletcher Henderson began to build up the larger ensembles which led to the big "swing" bands of the thirties.

Jelly Roll Morton

Jerome Kern
1885-1945

Jerome Kern always loved to tell how he had finally persuaded his father to let him become a composer. Although he grew up in a musical family, showed an early aptitude for the piano, began composing while still in high school and then spent several months studying in Germany, music was still considered a somewhat disreputable career and the elder Kern wanted him to find a place in his Newark department store. He quickly fumbled his way free. Drowsing during a produce auction where he represented the firm, he accidentally nodded at the wrong moment and found he had purchased an unusable quantity of prunes. Sent to the Bronx to sign a contract for two pianos, he partook of a heavy wine and pasta lunch with the Italian manufacturers and then let himself order two hundred. It was obviously time to let him go his own way.

Once he did, Kern demonstrated a precise, businesslike approach to composing almost unique in American musical history. He resumed his formal music studies, published several short piano pieces and went to work for New York music publishers, first doing clerical work, then "plugging" new songs (playing them in stores to promote sheet-music sales). By 1904 he was well enough connected in the business to have several of his songs included in a Broadway show.

For the next decade most of Kern's songs originally appeared as extra material in other composers' shows. At a time when English musicals and reviews largely dominated the American stage, he crossed the Atlantic many times and became adept at adapting English works for American audiences and vice versa. (He also acquired an English wife and a number of English mannerisms). He had begun to produce entire shows of his own material when World War I cut off the flow of European music (German operas had also been very popular). By the end of the war a new style of American musical had developed and Kern was widely considered its finest composer.

He managed to achieve this position through a series of shows that were only moderately successful and with few hit songs of his own; whatever they thought of the rest of the show, the critics usually praised the simple, lilting charm of his music. After 1920, however, Kern had both hit shows and hit songs aplenty, climaxing in *Show Boat* (featuring "Ol' Man River") and *Roberta* (featuring "Smoke Gets in Your Eyes"). Toward the end of the decade he began to compose for movie musicals; the ones which starred Fred Astaire included songs like "I Won't Dance," "A Fine Romance" and "The Way You Look Tonight."

As he rose in the musical world, Kern became increasingly demanding of those he worked with (he insisted that his lyricists follow his suggestions and resisted producers' attempts to change his music), and never established a long-running professional collaboration as did George and Ira Gershwin or Rodgers and Hart. But if he was hard to work with many of his colleagues must still have regarded him as the greatest American songwriter ever.

Jerome Kern

Cole Porter
1891-1964

The American musical theater squeezed together a number of not always compatible traditions: blackface "minstrel" song and dance shows; low-level "burlesques" of popular plays; and romantic European operettas. The first two tended to make fun of all levels of society, while the operettas glamorized the emotional conflicts of an almost imaginary upper class. As a distinctive American style of musical play took shape toward the end of the nineteenth century, it was the operetta strain that produced the sentimental songs that became the musical hits with the general public. Yet many of the men who composed these songs were lower-class sons of recent immigrant groups—English, Irish and Germans at first, then eastern European Jews. Cole Porter was the first great American theater composer whose upper class fantasies actually reflected his own background.

The son of a moderately successful Indiana pharmacist, Porter was also the grandson of J. O. Cole, who had made a fortune in the California Gold rush and increased it by careful investments back home. He attended Eastern private schools and then Yale, where he was supposed to prepare for a career in business or the law. But he devoted most of his time there to writing songs for college theatricals, which delighted students and alumni and provided several of Yale's most famous football songs (including "Bingo Eli Yale" and "The Bulldog Song"). After a brief stint at Harvard Law School, he threw himself wholeheartedly into the theater, writing entire shows for Yale associations while placing a few songs in major Broadway productions. He had the means to accomplish all this while beginning to make his way in French society.

In 1919 Porter married the wealthy divorcée Linda Thomas, whose extra income allowed him the freedom to write whatever he wanted. But it was just at this time that his songs—he now wrote both music and words—began to make a hit. He wrote songs for dozens of musicals throughout the twenties and thirties. Though these often failed to make much of an impression at first hearing, audiences frequently found that Porter's catchy tunes and witty, sophisticated lyrics stuck in their minds. "Let's Do it," "You Do Something to Me," "Night and Day," "I Get a Kick Out of You," "You're the Top," "Anything Goes," "Begin the Beguine" and many others perfectly expressed the hedonistic, yet sometimes melancholy, tenor of high society life between the World Wars.

A horseriding accident in 1937 shattered both of Porter's legs and sharply curtailed both his social and musical activity. He would be in pain for the rest of his life, but he fought his way back, writing such widely divergent songs as "Don't Fence Me In" and "You'd Be So Nice to Come Home To" and turning out his finest musical, *Kiss Me Kate,* in 1948. Linda's death in 1954 and the amputation of his right leg four years later had a much more dampening effect. His best songs of the 1950s ("I Love Paris" and "True Love" among them) were far gentler and more sentimental than the ones which had first made him famous.

Cole Porter

Irving Berlin
1888-1989

In the early years of the twentieth century, New York and many other American cities teemed with often self-educated musicians and composers eager to make a hit. Before the spread of the phonograph, the radio or the movies, they counted on selling their songs to music-hall and theater producers or to the thousands of sheet-music publishers who made up the mythical "Tin Pan Alley." Most of these men could bang out their tunes with some authority on an upright piano. Irving Berlin, who became the most prolific and successful popular composer of the century, couldn't even do that: for most of his career he either sang or hummed his songs to musical secretaries who then committed them to paper.

But then he never intended to become a songwriter. Born Israel Baline in Russia, he came to New York with his Jewish parents at four and lost his cantor father at eight. Like his older siblings, he hit the streets to help support the family, first as a newsboy and then—after temporarily running away from home—as a singing waiter in the bars of the Bowery. From singing other people's songs, it was a short step to writing his own.

Baline became Berlin through a misprint on the cover of his first published song. The seventeen-year-old had only written the lyrics to that one and for the next few years he continued to seek out more experienced composers to set music to his words. But he dictated his own tunes when no other composer was available. Both he and his publisher gradually noticed that the songs for which he wrote both words and music were more popular than his collaborations.

"Alexander's Ragtime Band" made Berlin world famous in 1911; after that there was no stopping him. In the next fifty years he published over 1,500 songs. Writing for Broadway revues, musical comedies, army benefits, movies, sheet-music publication and, eventually, records, he composed in an almost unbelievable variety of styles. He could do patriotic odes ("God Bless America"), humorous ditties (Oh, How I Hate to Get Up in the Morning"), sophisticated dances ("Putting on the Ritz," "Top Hat, White Tie and Tails," "Cheek to Cheek"); he could be upbeat ("Blue Skies"), torchy ("Heat Wave"), nostalgic ("White Christmas"), and even, occasionally, cynical ("Lady of the Evening").

As he prospered, Berlin built his own Broadway theater and established his own publishing company. In time he learned to compose on the piano—somewhat. Even on the specially constructed instrument he travelled with—it had a special lever for changing keys—he picked out all his tunes only on the black keys. But, in spite of his technical limitations, his musical inventiveness seemed to grow with every year. *Annie Get Your Gun*, which he wrote at fifty-eight, was easily his most complex and well-fashioned musical; his final, less successful, musical, *Mr. President*, appeared when he was seventy-four. Although he became quite reclusive during the last years of his life, Berlin surely took pleasure in the undiminished popularity of his songs.

Ethel Merman, Richard Rodgers & Irving Berlin

William Grant Still
1895-1978

William Grant Still, the "dean of Afro-American composers," as he was often called in his own lifetime, was born in Woodville, Mississippi to schoolteacher parents. His father, the village bandleader as well, died soon after, and his mother, a woman both musical and artistic, took him to Little Rock, Arkansas, where he grew up. He began to learn the violin, and was first exposed to opera, a life long love, by his stepfather's records. In college, though, he initially studied science, for his mother wanted him to become a doctor.

But Still was irresistibly drawn back to music, and was soon playing in combos and working as an arranger, at one time for the legendary W. C. Handy. He furthered his musical studies at Oberlin, then privately in Boston with George Chadwick, and finally with Edgar Varèse in New York. The latter's avant-garde influence was felt for a time in Still's composition, but he found his own voice in becoming the musical voice of his people's experience. Over the next few decades he wrote the first symphony by a black man to be performed by a major orchestra, and the first opera produced by a major company. The *Afro-American Symphony* of 1930, generally considered his masterpiece, incorporated melodies with a strong blues feeling. The opera *Troubled Island* of 1938, with a libretto by Still's wife Verna and the great black American poet Langston Hughes, told the story of the liberation of Haiti while evoking the music of that island.

Still settled in southern California, and did arrangements for big bands, including Artie Shaw's, also composing, arranging and conducting for radio, movies (including *Pennies from Heaven* and *Lost Horizon*) and later television (*Gunsmoke* and *Perry Mason*). All the while he was busily composing serious music as well, and his lifetime output included six operas, five symphonies, four ballets, numerous other orchestral and chamber pieces, and several cantatas, the first of which, *And They Lynched Him on a Tree*, employed two choruses, black and white, in a moving plea for racial justice and harmony.

Walter Piston
1894-1976

For nearly half a century, the most rigorous and dedicated creator of pure, instrumental music in the United States was Walter Piston. Aaron Copland said his works constituted a challenge to every other American composer.

Piston was born in Rockland, Maine, and as a boy taught himself to play violin and piano. But in his early years he seemed destined for a career in the visual arts. After graduating from high school in Boston, he worked as a mechanical draftsman, and then entered the Massachusetts Normal Art School, where he met his future wife, the painter Kathryn Nason. At the same time, he was playing in cafés and dance halls, and towards the end of World War I he joined the navy, playing saxophone in a band based at MIT. By the time of his discharge, Piston knew that music was his calling. At the age of twenty-six he enrolled at Harvard, graduating with honors four years later. Two years of study in Paris followed, with Nadia Boulanger and Paul Dukas.

Upon his return to the United States, Piston taught music at Harvard; he remained on the faculty until 1960. Leonard Bernstein and Elliott Carter were his most celebrated students, but for several generations most aspiring composers have studied with Walter Piston through the medium of his vastly influential textbooks on harmony, counterpoint and orchestration.

Piston's music was almost completely instrumental, strongly neoclassical in structure and feeling, and very rarely programmatic, though an exception, the witty and colorful ballet *The Incredible Flutist*, became his most popular work. Among his other major compositions were the suite *Three New England Sketches*, five string quartets, and eight symphonies, two of which won the Pulitzer Prize. Of his work, his student Elliott Carter observed "...(it) helps us to keep our mind on the durable and the most satisfying aspects of the art of music and by making them live gives us hope that the qualities of integrity and reason are still with us."

Roger Sessions
1896-1985

In the decades following World War II the arts in the United States sank deep roots in the academy; for the first time a poet's or painter's vision was most probably shaped by a university education, and results were often incomprehensible to the public. Academic composers, in particular, embracing the thorny, difficult theories of Schönberg and Webern, produced cerebral works more readily appreciated by their colleagues than by a lay audience. Dozens of them were the students of Roger Sessions, the most influential teacher of composition in America for half a century. Sessions himself composed dense and challenging music less often heard in the concert hall than that of the minimalists and "neo-romantics" who came after him, but he was nonetheless a towering presence on the musical landscape, a "composer's composer" and the most untiring champion of new music in our time.

Sessions was musically and academically precocious. Born in Brooklyn of Yankee parents, he composed his first opera as a child and entered Harvard at fourteen. He then studied at Yale, and privately with the Swiss-American composer Ernest Bloch, under whose influence he composed music for the play *The Black Maskers*. The 1923 suite he extracted from it established his reputation. Other of his early works reflected the influence of Stravinsky. At this time he assumed a post at Smith College and remained in an academic environment for much of the rest of his life, teaching at Princeton, Berkeley, Harvard and Juilliard.

Sessions began to arrive at his mature style by the late 1930s. From about 1950 on his work incorporated elements of twelve-tone music. His later years were particularly fruitful; he composed seven of his nine symphonies after he was sixty. Sessions never sought to create a self-consciously American music, and his internationalist and humanistic perspective informs his largest work, the opera *Montezuma*, a monumental meditation on the conquest of Mexico.

Howard Hanson
1896-1981

American classical music came of age in the 1920s. Since then music education has been widespread and sophisticated enough for Americans to appreciate the full range of European tradition, without becoming slavish followers of German romanticism or any other school. At the same time, they've had the chance to discover the richness of their native musical heritage and to trust their own innovations. Howard Hanson was for many years one of the leading forces in both of these developments.

As a composer he used traditional, often romantic, forms to express a distinctly American temperament; as a conductor and educator he encouraged some of the most advanced contemporary composers. Born in Wahoo, Nebraska, to Swedish immigrant parents, Hanson found his place in music at an early age. He became professor of theory and composition at the College of the Pacific in 1916, dean of the school's Conservatory of Fine Arts in 1919, winner of the Prix de Rome in 1921 and director of the Eastman School of Music in Rochester, New York, in 1924. During his forty years at Eastman, he led the American Music Festival in the performance of some 1,500 new works by some 700 composers. His many years of teaching and conducting culminated in the 1960 book *Harmonic Materials of Modern Music*, in which he tried to "analyze *all* the possibilities of the twelve-tone scale."

Though more traditional in style than that of many of his contemporaries, Hanson's own music was, he said a "direct expression of my own emotional reactions." It could be lyrical, playful, austere or melancholy. Perhaps because of his Scandinavian ancestry, perhaps because of the restrained, economical way he handled powerful musical emotions, some critics labelled him the "American Sibelius." In addition to his popular second ("Romantic") symphony of 1930 he wrote four other symphonies, the opera *Merry Mount* and numerous orchestral, choral and chamber works.

Virgil Thomson
1896-1989

American musicians who travelled to Europe to study during the 1920s were in for a surprise. The most talented young European composers, it seemed, were constructing some of their most advanced works on patterns they'd taken from American music. And it wasn't famous American composers like MacDowell they were copying, either; it was the nearly anonymous teams of African -Americans who were still in the process of creating the new style called jazz.

Some of the staider young Americans found this situation baffling. But Virgil Thomson, who arrived in Paris in 1921 to study with Nadia Boulanger, was not a man to be baffled by anything. The musical prodigy of Kansas City, Missouri, he had served in the Army Air Corps during World War I, then gone on to Harvard, where he shone both as a musician and a writer. After his first year in Paris, he returned to Harvard and a short series of post-graduate jobs. Preferring to "starve where the food is good," he went back to Paris in 1925. This time he combined the influence of the simple, off-beat music of the French composer Erik Satie with the linguistic experiments of the expatriate American writer Gertrude Stein. He set her abstract, stylized lyrics to equally stylized, mockingly rhetorical music, cast the piece for an all-black company and came up with the opera *Four Saints in Three Acts*.

A huge success when it opened in New York in 1934, *Four Saints* brought Thomson instant fame and won him commissions for other pieces either reflecting ordinary American life or using the straightforward style, often reminiscent of folk and popular music, which he had made his own. In addition to *The Mother of Us All*, a second opera with a Stein libretto based on the life of Susan B. Anthony, he wrote the music for *The Plough that Broke the Plains*, *The River*, *Louisiana Story* and other films; incidental music for many plays; choral and orchestral works; and several ballets, among them one called *Filling Station*. Over the years he also composed a series of musical portraits, mostly for piano, "sketched from life," and each intended to be a recognizable likeness of its subject.

Thomson's criticism was at least as influential as his music and many consider him the greatest American music critic. Both in his books and during his fourteen-year stint at the *New York Herald Tribune* he always championed the new, the fresh and the unusual.

Young Virgil Thompson

Jimmie Rodgers
1897-1933

The rural counties of the Deep Southern states were for many years the poorest regions in America. Most of the people who lived there never got to experience the operas, minstrel shows and marching bands which regularly appeared in the big cities. They rarely even got to see the sheet music of the latest big hit tunes. But they did have their own music. They had preserved the songs which their ancestors had brought over from England, Ireland and Scotland—or, almost as often, from Africa—and slowly adapted them to new living conditions and a new set of musical instruments. In many isolated towns it seemed that almost everyone could sing or play (on fiddle, banjo, or guitar) an immense repertory of tunes.

By the early 1900s the best of these performers were beginning to make a living travelling a circuit of nearby towns. In the early 1920s they started to reach larger audiences through radio programs and phonograph records. As the big-city record companies discovered that there was a market for "hillbilly" music, they rushed to sign up all the local favorites they could find. In early August 1927 one record scout hired both the Carter Family and Jimmie Rodgers. Between them, Rodgers and the Carters almost completely defined what later came to be called "country music."

A. P. Carter, his wife Sara and his sister-in-law Maybelle sang traditional songs in the traditional manner, accompanying their broad nasal harmonies with sharp banjo, guitar and autoharp playing. Jimmie Rodgers brought together almost every tradition which had ever passed through the South and then added a few tricks of his own. The son of a Mississippi railroad worker, he had lost his mother when he was only four and then followed his father on jobs all over the South. His travels exposed him not only to the current styles of city-based popular music, but also to the itinerant troupes of Swiss yodelers, Hawaiian steel guitarists and other novelty performers who were then in vogue. Most important of all, he spent long periods with African-American railroad workers, who taught him banjo and guitar and a good number of their songs.

Rodgers made little practical use of his unusual musical education until tuberculosis forced him to retire from the railroads in 1925. In the next two years he played in a number of moderately successful groups. But then, within six months of making his first records, he became the most popular musician in the South. Although his high clear voice and his individual guitar style—he was one of the first whites to adopt black techniques—explained part of his appeal, he owed most of his sudden popularity to his unique "blue yodel." This was a completely new kind of high-spirited wail which he tossed out after each stanza of a traditional blues song.

In spite of his continued bad health, Rodgers toured and recorded until the last few days of his life. Resettled in a dry part of Texas, he presented himself as a jaunty young Southern gentleman who could give his audiences whatever they wanted. His songs, many of which he wrote himself, could be sentimental, humorous, maudlin or even rowdy; they always seemed totally sincere. One admirer has estimated that his style was the inspiration for seventy-five percent of all later country singers.

Jimmie Rodgers

Henry Cowell
1897-1965

Henry Cowell's parents started him on violin lessons at the age of five. The stress their expectations aroused in him began to affect his health until he had to stop. But music was in his blood by then and he decided to become a composer instead, producing his first substantial piece, a setting of a poem by Henry Longfellow, when he was eleven. His parents had divorced by that time and he and his mother had left his California birthplace to try their luck in the Midwest and East. While she made her way as a writer, he continued to compose, picking up inspiration from the folk songs and dances (Irish especially) he heard among his relatives. Returning to California in 1910, he earned enough at odd jobs to buy a piano and settled into fifty years of unabashedly enthusiastic music-making.

Cowell's music was radically new and different. Though he took much of his inspiration from Irish sources, he often found it easier to express certain emotions or events by depressing a handful (or forearmful) of piano keys at once (he called these tone-clusters) or by moving to the side of the piano and plucking the strings with his fingers. Since he had almost no formal education, he didn't even know when he was breaking the rules of conventional music; he simply tried to recreate the world he was experiencing with the sounds (American, Irish, Oriental or modern urban) he had experienced. He had already written some one hundred pieces when he gave his first San Francisco piano concert in 1914.

Cowell did attempt some formal musical training that same year, studying with Charles Seeger at the University of California at Berkeley and later briefly in New York. But his theories of music, like his compositions and performances, came more from his own interaction with the modern world than from any clear-cut tradition. In later years he travelled extensively, both as a performer and as a diligent student of world music. As his mastery of his own personal idiom increased, he strove more and more to incorporate folk-tunes, old American hymns (some by William Billings) and elements of Asian and African music into his work. Kind and trusting in almost all aspects of his life, he devoted much of his time to promoting the work of neglected pioneers like Charles Ives; his many students included John Cage, Lou Harrison and the already brilliantly successful George Gershwin.

Roy Harris
1898-1979

A baseball manager supposedly wrote to Roy Harris after hearing his Third Symphony. "If I had pitchers who could pitch as strongly as you do in your symphony," he insisted, "my worries would be over."

That was in the late thirties, when Americans were discovering the beauties of their popular culture and American composers were incorporating traditional tunes and rhythms in their music. Of the many composers who made use of folk elements in their work, Harris and Aaron Copland were by far the most successful.

Harris certainly had the proper credentials for the job. Born on Lincoln's Birthday in Lincoln County, Oklahoma, he spent his early years farming, both there and in the Los Angeles area and worked four years as a truck driver for a dairy before entering the University of California. While concentrating on philosophy and economics, he began studying harmony and then continued with private classes in composition. He caught on quickly—his Andante for orchestra was performed at a Hollywood Bowl concert in 1926—then headed East to refine his skills.

Though he spent some time in Paris studying European music with Nadia Boulanger, Harris usually structured his works, which included sixteen symphonies, around the irregular cadences and flatted harmonies which he thought expressed the particularly American moods of "noisy ribaldry...sadness...(and) groping earnestness." He probably reached his creative peak in the years just before World War II, when those moods were still largely intact.

George Gershwin
1898-1937

In April, 1925 George Gershwin signed a contract with the New York Symphony Orchestra to compose and perform a piano concerto. He then reportedly had to find out exactly what a concerto was and buy a book explaining how to score music for an orchestra. Though he was, at twenty-six, one of the rising stars of American popular music, Gershwin had only a rudimentary knowledge of complex musical forms. But he was so ambitious and so supremely self-confident that he assumed he could conquer the concert hall as easily as he had the music hall.

The son of Russian Jewish immigrants, Gershwin had grown up in Brooklyn and on the lower East Side of Manhattan. An outgoing, energetic, athletic boy, he ignored his schoolwork as much as possible and seemed to have no intellectual or artistic interests. It was only when his parents bought a piano for his older brother Ira in 1910 that his innate musical talent came to light. He learned so quickly that he was able to leave school four years later to become a pianist and song plugger for a Tin Pan Alley publisher.

Gershwin rose just as quickly in the music business, publishing his first song and contributing to a Broadway musical when only seventeen. By the early 1920s his catchy, melodious tunes had appeared in dozens of shows; one of them, "Swanee," had become the trademark of the great singer Al Jolson. They were also gaining the attention of classical musicians and composers, who were just beginning to appreciate American jazz. After the spectacular success of his *Rhapsody in Blue* for jazz band and piano in 1924, he suddenly found himself lionized as the one composer whose music appealed to both popular and classical audiences.

Although his songs weren't really jazz, they mixed African-American rhythms with Jewish music hall harmonies and the melodic structure of traditional American popular music in an easy, infectious way that seemed entirely new. Especially after his brother Ira became his chief lyricist and the two began picking out tunes together on the family piano, such Gershwin songs as "The Man I Love," "S'Wonderful," "Fascinating Rhythm, " "Someone to Watch Over Me" and "I Got Rhythm" were a regular feature of every Broadway season.

But Gershwin always hankered after the greater respectability of classical music. His Piano Concerto—almost as successful as the *Rhapsody*—was followed by the large orchestral pieces *An American In Paris* and the *Second Rhapsody*. As Early as 1926, he determined to make an opera of DuBose Hayword's novel *Porgy*, set in the black community of "Catfish Row" in Charleston, South Carolina. Though *Porgy and Bess* was only a moderate success when it appeared in 1935, it contained both his most masterful essay at classical form and his finest collection of individual songs ("Summertime," "I Got Plenty of Nuttin'," and "It Ain't Necessarily So" among them). It is now considered the greatest American opera.

Ever more at ease in both the popular and classical styles, and still gaining in technical command, Gershwin died suddenly of a brain tumor at the age of thirty-eight. It was a tragic loss for American music; of him it might be said as it was of Schubert: the art of music here entombed a rich possession but even far fairer hopes.

Gershwin's Dog Tony

George Gershwin

Edward Kennedy (Duke) Ellington
1899-1974

Some composers create their music on a piano, some on paper, some these days on a synthesizer or computer. Duke Ellington wrote his music in many, often uncomfortable locations—in bars and cars and trains and restaurants—but that was only his way of keeping track of his ideas. He actually composed with his orchestra itself, like a painter with his palette and brushes or an organist with his dozens of stops.

No one else in American history ever matched this deceptively smooth style of composition, but, then, no one else in American music ever had that kind of orchestra. Ellington led the same organization for nearly fifty of the most eventful years in jazz history; several of his players stayed with the group for over forty years. "Writing" a new piece for them might consist of handing a scrap of paper with a few notes on it to trumpeter Cootie Williams or offering some general verbal suggestions to alto saxophonist Johnny Hodges. The orchestra then proceeded to produce the new work.

It wasn't the sort of life anyone would have predicted for him. Growing up in Washington, D.C. in the early 1900s, he was the son of a middle-class African-American family, the kind that aspired to a conventional, European-style way of life, and he showed more aptitude for painting than anything else. In his early teens, however, he discovered that his piano playing attracted more girls than his artwork. By his late teens he was earning enough money painting signs, playing music and booking other musical groups to marry and buy a house. His commanding presence and stylish manners had already earned him the nickname "Duke."

Then he followed friends to New York City, where the new jazz style that had originated in New Orleans was gradually taking over. By 1927 Ellington had become leader of a band whose growly "jungle sound," largely produced by muted trumpets and trombones, won them a job at the celebrated Cotton Club and a nationwide radio audience. Relying on the talents of this group, he began to work up short pieces like "Creole Love Call," "Black and Tan Fantasy" and "Mood Indigo."

By the 1930s Ellington had evolved the smoother, more symphonic style which he maintained for the rest of his life. At the peak of his commercial success, with new talents like bassist Jimmy Blanton and arranger Billy Strayhorn streaming into his organization, he came up with such compositions as "Sophisticated Lady," "Solitude," "Ko-Ko" and "Don't Get Around Much Anymore," while other band members produced "Perdido," "Caravan" and "Take the A Train."

Big band jazz almost disappeared after World War II, but Ellington managed to keep his group together and staged a major comeback at the 1956 Newport Jazz Festival. By then he was taking himself more seriously as a composer and had begun to write longer "suites" like *Black, Brown and Beige* and, eventually, three "sacred concerts." World tours enhanced his reputation as the most important single force in jazz history and kept him busy working until the last days of his life.

Duke Ellington

Aaron Copland
1900-1990

Becoming a composer in America around 1920 was not an easy matter. Though a city like New York boasted several symphony orchestras and dozens of theaters, the music they performed was usually either European or based on European models. Even the music halls tended to recreate the Old World styles of the groups of immigrants they catered to, whether they were English, German, Irish, Jewish, African or a mixture of nationalities. The best teachers, the ones the most serious students of music sought out, were almost all either European or European-trained.

Aaron Copland was as serious a student of music as you could find. After discovering the piano when he was eleven, he worked his way through the best teachers in Brooklyn, where his Russian Jewish parents ran a department store, and Manhattan in the next ten years. Then he went on to Paris, where he became one of the first American students of Nadia Boulanger, probably the most important music teacher of the twentieth century. Her insistence on giving equal attention to the broad sweep and the intricate details of composition reinforced Copland's austere, precise and fluent style.

After he returned to New York in 1924, Copland quickly made his name in classical music circles. His models were clearly European avant-garde—Stravinsky, Schönberg, Hindemith. Even when he included jazz elements in his *Music for the Theatre* of 1925, his work was more in the style of Stravinsky or Milhaud than of an American natural like George Gershwin.

The Great Crash of 1929 changed all that. With millions of people out of work, it no longer seemed possible to compose music for the appreciation of small cultivated audiences. Like many other artists and musicians, Copland began to examine the life and art of ordinary people, both past and present. Along the way he found a rich new source of musical inspiration.

After the success of *El Salón México*, a piece which combined Mexican popular tunes to suggest the atmosphere of a Mexican dance hall, in 1935, Copland produced a number of works based on folklore or everyday life. Most notable were the ballets *Billy the Kid, Rodeo,* and *Appalachian Spring*; the film scores *Of Mice and Men, Our Town* and *The Red Pony*; and the Third Symphony, which included a movement based on the *Fanfare for the Common Man*. For a composer who spent most of his life in or near large cities, they expressed an unusually strong feeling, almost a longing, for rural life.

The prosperity and Cold War atmosphere which followed World War II reduced American social consciousness once more. After 1950, Copland returned to more formalistic, less immediately accessible music. He also began a second career as a music educator, especially as director of the Berkshire Music Festival at Tanglewood, Massachusetts. But he continued to write some pieces in a simpler, more folk-oriented style, most notably the opera *The Tender Land*. Together with the masterpieces of the previous fifteen years, they confirmed his place as the most popular American classical composer of the century.

Aaron Copland

Samuel Barber
1910-1981

Only half-a-generation younger than Thomson and Hanson, Samuel Barber seemed to grow effortlessly along with American music. Son of a prosperous Pennsylvania doctor, nephew of the celebrated contralto Louise Homer, he knew he wanted to be a composer by the time he was nine and wrote his first opera at ten. One of the first students at the Curtis Institute of Music in Philadelphia, he was allowed to major in composition, piano and voice; with excellent teachers in all three areas, he came to an early mastery of vocal and instrumental technique. His gift for expressive melodies then flowered unimpaired.

Early critical success confirmed Barber's promise and gave him enough security to devote himself to composition. During the 1930s he won a Pulitzer Fellowship and the Prix de Rome and composed some of his most important works, including *Dover Beach* for baritone and strings, the *Overture to the School for Scandal* and the *Adagio for Strings*. Originally the slow movement of his second string quartet, the *Adagio* was orchestrated by Barber at the request of Arturo Toscanini. This hauntingly beautiful evocation of sorrow became and has remained one of the most popular of all American classical compositions. After World War II, which he spent in the Army Air Corps, he shared a house near Mt. Kisco, New York, with fellow-composer Gian Carlo Menotti. Each man had his own wing, where he could work without hearing the other.

Barber's post-war work retained its melodic flow while becoming harmonically more adventurous and emotionally more intense. Though never as popular as his earlier music, pieces like *Medea's Meditation and Dance of Vengeance* (from the ballet *Medea*), *Knoxville: Summer of 1915* for soprano and orchestra and the Sonata in E-Flat Major for piano won wide critical acclaim. His opera *Vanessa* won the Pulitzer Prize for music in 1958, as did his Piano Concerto in 1963. He was generally considered the most important American composer of the 1950s and 1960s and was commissioned to write the grandiose opera *Antony and Cleopatra* for the opening of the new Metropolitan Opera House at Lincoln Center in New York in 1966.

Richard Rodgers
1902-1979

As late as the 1930s, most Broadway musicals were still almost haphazard collections of songs and dances. Producers often constructed their shows around a few famous performers, contracted with successful songwriters to tailor musical numbers to the stars' abilities, and finally hired a writer or two to concoct a plot that would hold it all together. Though a number of composers—Kern, Gershwin and Porter among them—tried to make more sense out of what were often simply musical revues, it was Richard Rodgers who really created the modern American musical play.

You could almost say that he did it twice, with two different partners, in two different styles. The son of a prosperous New York doctor, he had begun writing Kern-inspired songs while still in high school. In 1918 he started passing some of his tunes to the budding lyricist Lorenz Hart. Seven years older than Rodgers, Hart had a witty, sometimes cynical attitude that smoothly fit the flamboyant theatrical style of the time. But both men wanted to go beyond the hackneyed plots and situations that were then common.

After a number of false starts, Rodgers and Hart were by 1925 so successful that they could safely experiment with the kind of songs and stories that appealed to them. In shows like *On Your Toes, Babes in Arms, The Boys From Syracuse* and *Pal Joey,* they produced tighter, more realistic and more engaging musicals than anyone before, while still providing the hit songs ("My Funny Valentine," "The Lady is a Tramp," "This Can't Be Love," "Bewitched, Bothered and Bewildered" and others) that their audiences expected.

But Hart's sensitive lyrics reflected his own personal difficulties. He slowly withdrew from the partnership several years before his premature death in 1943. For his new lyricist, Rodgers chose a man who was almost Hart's exact opposite. Oscar Hammerstein II had worked with Friml, Romburg, Gershwin and Kern (most notably in *Showboat*). His lyrics, of which "Ol' Man River" was probably the best-known, had a solid, craftsmanlike, sometimes sentimental, cast, with little of Hart's inspired foolery.

But Hammerstein was also willing to take chances. For their first project together, he and Rodgers adapted a ten-year-old "folk play" no other songwriters would even consider. With its rousing songs ("People Will Say We're in Love," "Oh, What a Beautiful Mornin'," "The Surrey With the Fringe on Top") and nearly seamless fusion of story and music, *Oklahoma!* was such a resounding success when it opened in 1943 that it almost killed the old-style musical pastiche.

For the next two decades, Rodgers and Hammerstein musicals like *Carousel, South Pacific, The King and I, Flower Drum Song* and *The Sound of Music* completely dominated Broadway, bringing the American musical to its peak. Rodgers also wrote the music for the TV documentary series *Victory at Sea* and wrote his own lyrics for the musical *No Strings* after Hammerstein's death. But he will be best remembered for the songs he crafted with his two dissimilar partners.

Richard Rodgers

Elliott Carter
1908-

By the time Elliot Carter graduated from Harvard in 1930, going to Paris to study with Nadia Boulanger was almost a rite of passage for promising young American composers. For many of them working with Boulanger provided an opportunity to smooth out their rough American musical edges. For Carter, who came to music after studying literature, it reinforced his natural tendency toward sensitive, often mathematically precise, complexity.

Like many composers who began serious work in the thirties, Carter used explicitly American themes in such early pieces as the ballet *Pocahontas*. But he was usually more interested in the formal possibilities of a particular composition than in its non-musical content. After World War II he gave freer rein to his penchant for complex, interlocking rhythms. Especially in his string quartets and concertos he came to be recognized as the most consistently successful of the composers who were trying to find new possibilities in traditional forms.

While contemporaries like John Cage often gave performers only very sketchy indications of what to play in their pieces, Carter sometimes achieved the same sense of freedom using carefully worked out rhythms and melodies. In his quartets he would give each player what seemed to be a completely independent part, with its own intricate rhythms, yet balance them all so well that they formed an integrated whole. Within his vast, intellectually demanding structures he nonetheless managed to express a complete range of emotional reactions to the passing world: passion, humor, solemnity and a melting sadness.

Alan Hovhaness
1911-

East is East and West is West, and never the twain shall meet. So said Rudyard Kipling. But East and West have met and borne fruit in the music of Alan Hovhaness for over half a century. When the University of Rochester awarded him an honorary doctorate in music in 1959, the citation stated: "The despair of Kipling is the glory of Hovhaness."

Born in Somerville, Massachusetts of an Armenian father and Scottish mother, Hovhaness began composing as a child, writing two operas by the age of thirteen. He studied at the New England Conservatory and achieved early success with compositions in the late Romantic idiom of Sibelius. In his early forties he fell under the spell of Eastern music, and, dissatisfied with his work till then, burned several hundred scores, including seven symphonies.

At this point Hovhaness began to explore his own Armenian heritage, making an intensive study of its ancient liturgical music. He proceeded to explore the musics of other Near and Middle Eastern cultures, and then, after attending a performance in Boston by Uday Shankar's company of musicians and dancers, turned to India for inspiration. In the years that followed, spurred by insatiable musical curiosity and his lifelong spiritual and mystical temperament, he moved on to China, Korea and Japan. All the while he was composing as prolifically as anyone has in our time. He combined his Eastern sources with Western techniques, often medieval or Renaissance in derivation, to produce works of haunting beauty, and nearly always religious feeling.

Among the many hundreds of compositions by Hovhaness, one of the more popular and unusual is *And God Created Great Whales* (1970), which incorporates the taped songs of humpback whales. His single best known work is certainly the symphony *Mysterious Mountain*, premiered in 1955 by the Houston Symphony under Leopold Stokowski. Of it one critic observed that its real mystery was "...that it should be so simply, sweetly, innocently lovely in an age that has tried so terribly hard to avoid these impressions in music."

John Cage
1912-

"I wanted to find a way of making music that was free of the theory of harmony, " John Cage once said, "..and so I had to find a way of composing with noise." Not only the traditional systems of tonality, but even Arnold Schönberg's revolutionary twelve-tone method required composers to fit carefully chosen notes together in strictly regulated ways. When Cage decided to throw out all the regulations, many listeners thought he was producing nothing but noise. A few, who very slowly became many, thought his noises the most exciting music they had heard in years.

Cage himself thought they were experiments and he moved easily from experiment to experiment, not always noticing that he had left much of his audience behind. The son of a Los Angeles inventor, he got in the habit of improvising his life early on and never settled into any institutional patterns. After a few years at Pomona College in Claremont, he was still uncertain whether he wanted to be a painter, a writer or a composer. Travel in Europe and a year of study with Henry Cowell in New York inclined him toward music, but it was only when Schönberg insisted that he devote his life to music before accepting him as a student that he appeared to make up his mind.

Cage studied with Schönberg for over two years, but found even his seemingly discordant music too concerned with harmony—for which he himself had little feel—and in the late 1930s, influenced by Edgar Varèse, he began to experiment with percussion systems, dance rhythms and new kinds of sound. To increase the number of sounds available to a single performer, he wrote many pieces for "prepared piano," an instrument with miscellaneous objects such as clothespins, spoons and screws laid upon or stuck between its strings. Cage settled in New York in 1942 and began to work with the great choreographer Merce Cunningham, eventually becoming his music director. Cage composed without knowing the design of a given dance, and the dancers of the company in turn would not hear the music until the performance.

By this time he was one of the most respected experimental composers in America. But then he changed his technique. Inspired by his study of Indian, Chinese and Japanese philosophy, particularly Zen Buddhism and the *I Ching* (*Book of Changes*), Cage decided that it was not his job as composer to give performers immutable works to realize or interpret. He started instead to draft the broad outlines of pieces which would find their final form according to the whims of the performers—or sometimes of chance. In one of his *Imaginary Landscapes* the performers manipulated the reception and volume of twelve radios to produce a constantly varying set of sounds. For *Water Music* a deck of cards was employed to arrange the sounds of pouring water and radio static. *Music of Changes* was composed with the aid of the *I Ching*, the roll of two dice determining the choice of notes. *4'33"*, probably his most famous piece, simply required its performers to sit silently on the stage for four minutes and thirty-three seconds; the audience would experience the background sounds that occurred in that period.

John Cage

These "aleatory" or "chance" pieces gained Cage an international notoriety while losing him many of his earlier admirers. But he persisted throughout the 1950s and 1960s in taking himself out of his music and exposing his audiences more and more to natural and accidental patterns of sound. He worked with poets, painters, dancers, movie-makers and speakers to produce some of the first "happenings" (simultaneous but uncoordinated multi-media events) and was one of the pioneers of taped and electronic music. Yet he refused to take even these techniques too seriously. By the time the rest of the musical world caught up with him and acclaimed him as one of the great innovators of the twentieth century, he declared that he was now more interested in hunting mushrooms and playing chess.

Thelonious Monk
1917-1982

"The Jazz Age" is what F. Scott Fitzgerald called the period after World War I. The soulfulness and exuberance of jazz perfectly matched the cultural revolution which swept America during the giddy prosperity of the 1920s. "The Swing Age" would be a good name for the period from 1935 to 1945. In those years white bandleaders like Benny Goodman and Glen Miller smoothed out the big band style of jazz originated by blacks like Fletcher Henderson, Duke Ellington, Count Basie and Cab Calloway. Swing became so popular that it seemed likely to drown out the rougher, more instinctive styles of traditional jazz. Many African-Americans thought they were about to lose control of their most important contribution to American culture.

They reinvented it instead. Starting in the early forties, a group of young instrumentalists, almost all based in New York City, replaced the sleek, bland phrasing of the big swing bands with a tense, staccato style they called "bebop." Though they were all self-conscious artists, more interested in self-expression than either commercial success or simply having a good time playing music, they aimed to recreate the rhythmic excitement, the harmonic inventiveness and the improvisational freedom of early jazz. Some of them also wanted to make their way back to the African roots of their music, hoping eventually to craft a style which whites couldn't copy and spoil.

Thelonious Monk, who arrived in New York when he was four (he was born in North Carolina), got involved with bebop from the very beginning. He was house pianist at Minton's Playhouse in Harlem, the bebop headquarters, from the early forties and encouraged Bud Powell to become the first bebop piano star. But, unlike Powell, trumpeter Dizzy Gillespie or saxophonist Charlie Parker, Monk was less interested in fitting the angular thrust of bebop to traditional or improvised tunes than in creating entirely new structures worthy of the new style of playing. His compositions were far cooler, far more complex and at times far quirkier than anyone else's and they took a far longer time to catch on.

Where earlier jazz musicians had usually improvised variations on the basic melodies of the songs they were playing (and swing musicians had played carefully scored solo breaks), the bebop pioneers created new melodies by improvising on one or two chords of the original song. Monk carried this process to the extreme, crafting fairly long pieces from the rhythmic and harmonic variations he could derive from a few simple chords. His piano, which could carry both the rhythm and the harmony, was always the central focus of his work, but his compositions offered rich opportunities for almost any combination of instruments.

Though much of Monk's best work, including *'Round About Midnight, Humph* and *Criss Cross*, dated from the forties, he only achieved wide popularity in the late fifties. By then he was firmly set in his bebop ways, valuing his work far more than his audience and often seeming aloof and distant. He retired at the peak of his fame in the mid-seventies and spent the rest of his life in seclusion.

Thelonious Monk

Leonard Bernstein
1918-1990

In the fall of 1943 Leonard Bernstein was feeling very discouraged. At the age of twenty-five he seemed poised for a brilliant musical career. He was an outstanding pianist, excelling in both classical and popular styles; he had studied composition and conducting with some of the country's finest teachers at Harvard and the Curtis Institute of Music; he had recently been appointed assistant conductor for the New York Philharmonic Orchestra. Yet he never got to conduct the orchestra; his compositions went unheard; he had no recitals scheduled.

All that changed in less than a year. The day soprano Jennie Tourel included his song "I Hate Music" in one of her recitals, Bernstein had to suddenly substitute for famous conductor Bruno Walter at a nationally broadcast Philharmonic concert. His overwhelming success became a frontpage story in the New York newspapers. In the beginning of 1944 his *Jeremiah* symphony scored a triumph in Pittsburgh and New York. His *Fancy Free* was the biggest hit of the ballet season. *On the Town*, a musical derived from *Fancy Free*, was one of the biggest theatrical hits. Even his father, who had tried to cajole him from music into a part in his Boston beauty salon supply business, now acknowledged that "Lenny" was on the right track.

He rode it faster than many people would have thought possible. In the next dozen years Bernstein produced another symphony called *The Age of Anxiety*, the musicals *Wonderful Town* and *Candide*, the opera *Trouble in Tahiti*, music for the film *On the Waterfront* and a number of smaller works. He began conducting all over the world, making a spectacular opera debut with Milan's La Scala theater and starting a lifelong association with the Israel Philharmonic. He taught a lot as well, students at Brandeis University, musicians at the Tanglewood Music Festival, and the general public on the television show *Omnibus*, where his discussions of classical, jazz and popular music quickly made him the best-known musician in America.

1957 was his second miracle year. A few months after his musical *West Side Story* became one of the biggest hits in Broadway history, Bernstein was named co-director of the New York Philharmonic. Early in 1958 he became sole Musical Director of the orchestra, the first native-born American in its history. An expanded concert season, tours through North America and abroad and frequent television appearances brought the orchestra back from the brink of insolvency and made Bernstein's flamboyant, expressive conducting style familiar to larger audiences than any earlier conductor had ever reached.

When Bernstein resigned from the New York Philharmonic in 1969, he intended to start actively composing again. But by then he seemed to have written himself out. His 1971 *Mass* was a modest success, his 1976 musical *1600 Pennsylvania Avenue* a complete disaster. His conducting actually improved after he left New York, especially after he began to work regularly with the Vienna Philharmonic, with which he achieved outstanding performances of Haydn, Beethoven and Mahler. He died just five days after his retirement in 1990.

Maria Callas & Leonard Bernstein

Hank Williams
1923-1953

"Sincerity," Hank Williams once told an interviewer, was the secret of country music. "When a hillbilly sings a crazy song, he feels crazy. When he sings 'I Laid My Mother Away,' he sees her a-laying right there in the coffin."

No country singer was ever more sincere than Williams himself. His twangy, sinewy voice, which perfectly matched his long and bony body, could take his listeners romping, partying, rejoicing, grieving, despairing or just plain crying over a broken heart. In less than five years as a major performer he touched more people more deeply than even Jimmie Rodgers and brought country music to audiences which had always scorned it before.

His popularity reflected his sincerity; his sincerity reflected a difficult but ordinary life which seemed unlikely to produce a musician, let alone a star. Williams grew up in various southern Alabama country towns, the son of a feckless railroad worker who eventually left his family for a ten years' stay in a veterans' hospital and a much sturdier, more determined mother. He was always a scrambler, shining shoes and selling peanuts to earn a few cents, and he took to music with the same incentive in his early teens. Coached mostly by local amateurs and especially by an African-American street musician named Tee-tot, he was good enough to win an amateur music contest in Montgomery when he was only fourteen and then to find a spot on a local radio show.

From then on Williams was a professional musician. With his mother as his manager, he quickly learned how to form a band, how to get bookings in important locations, how to write appealing songs, how to communicate with his audience. With only a twenty-one month break as a shipyard worker during World War II (his frail physique kept him out of the army), he went from local to regional success. In 1946 he signed publishing and recording contracts; by 1949 he was well-known enough to appear on Nashville, Tennessee's Grand Ol' Opry radio program, the ultimate goal of all country performers. The Opry brought him a national audience for his live performances at the same time that songs like "Move It On Over," "I Saw the Light," "Honky Tonkin'," "I'm So Lonesome I Could Die" and "Why Don't You Love Me" were selling hundreds of thousands of records.

But then Williams began to fall apart, drinking too much, pushing himself too hard; his health began to decline and he became completely unreliable. His wife divorced him and the Opry fired him in 1952. Though he tried to reform, he was really past help. He died of a heart attack on New Year's Day of 1953.

Yet he continued to produce great songs through all his troubles (he never drank when either writing or recording), "Cold, Cold Heart," "Hey, Good Lookin'," "Jambalaya" and the ironic "I'll Never get Out of This World Alive" among them. In all the moods these songs encompassed, Williams knew how to find the simple tunes and words that would reach the greatest number of listeners.

Hank & Audrey Williams

Philip Glass
1937-

For most of the twentieth century American popular music—first jazz, then rock'n'roll—has enjoyed unprecedented influence in the rest of the world. But foreigners, Europeans in particular, have always hesitated to follow American models in large orchestral forms, what we conventionally call "classical" music. As much as they might admire a Gottschalk, a MacDowell or a Copland, they would never dream of copying them. John Cage, who seemed to repudiate the European classical tradition, was the first American composer whose innovations found a following abroad. Though he was too much of an individualist to form his own school, his work was a forerunner of minimalism, the first American movement to spread around the world.

Yet, perhaps because they were Americans, the minimalists drew much of their formal inspiration from abroad. Philip Glass, Steve Reich and Terry Riley, the three men who crystallized the movement in the 1960s and 1970s, all underwent their musical apprenticeship in New York City, but the techniques they evolved for carrying on the orchestral tradition Cage seemed to have demolished came from Asia and Africa rather than Europe. Glass, who was born in Baltimore, had completed a conventional training at New York's Juilliard School of Music before going on to study with Nadia Boulanger in Paris (the last of a long line of major American composers to do so). But he felt unreceptive to her academic approach, and at this time he met and studied Indian music with the great sitarist Ravi Shankar and tabla player Allah Rakha. He began to experiment with seemingly simple, repetitive pieces of music which would challenge their listeners to add their own responses rather than simply react to programmed musical emotions.

Professional musicians were at first hostile to this new style and Glass spent most of the late 1960s and early 1970s working with avant-garde theater in Paris and New York. As his music gradually took on large, more standardized and non-theatrical forms, he had to form his own group, the Philip Glass Ensemble, to get it performed. By 1974 he had completed a five-and-a-half hour piece, *Music in Twelve Parts*, which served as a sort of "catalogue" of his ideas on rhythm, repetition and musical structure. Though each part was based on a distinct rhythmic repetition, most listeners heard the whole as an interminable and almost unvarying pulse.

But accomplishing this formal framework for his music seemed to set Glass free and he returned to theatrical work for the massive opera *Einstein on the Beach* (1976), on which he collaborated with multi-media artist Robert Wilson. This time his repetitive pulse served as background for songs, speeches and dances following each other in a non-narrative, dream like sequence. *Einstein* was premiered at the Avignon Festival in France, toured the capitals of Europe triumphantly, and came home to sold-out performances at the Metropolitan Opera. The opera *Satyagraha* (1980) dealt with the early life of Mahatma Gandhi; the Sanskrit libretto was taken from the Hindu classic The *Bhagavad Gita*. A third "portrait opera," *Akhnaten* (1983), was about the monotheistic Egyptian pharaoh of the title. Glass then received commissions for the soundtracks for the movies *Koyaanisqatsi* and *Mishima* as well

Philip Glass

as a choral piece for the 1984 Olympics. In 1985 he collaborated with lyricists Paul Simon, David Byrne, Laurie Anderson and Suzanne Vega on the song cycle *Songs from Liquid Days*.

By the late 1980s Glass, and minimalism generally, still faced vocal critics and doubters, but he had gained a large and eager audience, especially in Europe. In 1988 alone he introduced three new works of musical theater. *The Fall of the House of Usher* was a chamber opera based on the tale by Poe. *The Making of the Representative for Planet 8* dramatized the English writer Doris Lessing's visionary science fiction. *1000 Airplanes on the Roof* was built around an actor's monologue. 1991's *Hydrogen Jukebox*, "heralding the fall of America and the loss of Earth" set twenty-one poems by Allen Ginsburg. Philip Glass's operas were now more widely performed than any since Puccini's.

Lou Harrison
1917-

Some twentieth-century composers, like Arnold Schönberg and his follow-ers, responded to the exhaustion of the European musical tradition by developing new sets of musical rules. Others, like Henry Cowell and Harry Partch, devised new ways of playing old instruments or created entirely new instruments. Still others, like John Cage, tried to do away with standard musical forms and instruments altogether. Lou Harrison, who early in his career worked with Cowell, Schönberg and Cage (though never at the same time!), took a bit from each of these approaches, then glued them all together with his own ideas about language, intonation and harmonious living.

A native of Portland, Oregon, Harrison has spent most of his life in northern California. In spite of his impressive musical mentors, he had to support himself for years working in flower shops, record stores, animal hospitals and various other jobs while writing and performing music on the side. As he became better known, he was able to travel abroad, especially to the Orient, to study non-Western styles and incorporate them in his own work. He used many Asian instruments, sometimes with his own modifications, and in the 1970s built two *gamelan* ensembles based on traditional Indonesian orchestras.

Often tuning his instruments in just intonation (the system used in Europe before the seventeenth century) and setting texts written in the universal language Esperanto, Harrison has produced a lyrical, often joyous body of music celebrating personal freedom, personal growth and the perpetual cycles of the natural world.